SPECIAL THANKS

Thanks to the people who helped create this workbook:

Maggie Baxter for writing the daily devotionals. Rudy Alexeeff, Abby Fahmi, Jessica Gatton, Amanda Nash and Matt Shetler for contributing to editing and content of the small group discussion guide and teaching outlines. Adam Hines for the layout and design.

THE GOOD LIFE SMALL GROUP SERIES

Rich Nathan and Vineyard Columbus

Published 2016 by
Vineyard Columbus
6000 Cooper Rd
Columbus, OH 43081
vineyardcolumbus.org
smallgroups@vineyardcolumbus.org

© 2016 by Vineyard Columbus

All rights reserved. No part of this publication may be reproduced, stored in a retrieval system or transmitted, in any form or by any means, electronic, mechanical, photocopying, recording or otherwise, without the prior written permission of the copyright owner.

Scripture quotations marked (NIV) are taken from the Holy Bible, New International Version®, NIV®. Copyright © 1973, 1978, 1984, 2011 by Biblica, Inc.™ Used by permission of Zondervan. All rights reserved worldwide. www.zondervan.com The "NIV" and "New International Version" are trademarks registered in the United States Patent and Trademark Office by Biblica, Inc.™

Scripture quotations from THE MESSAGE. Copyright © by Eugene H. Peterson 1993, 1994, 1995, 1996, 2000, 2001, 2002. Used by permission of Tyndale House Publishers, Inc.

Design and layout by States of Design, LLC

ISBN 978-0-9971238-0-7

CONTENTS

7 — WELCOME, HOW TO'S & RESOURCES

10 — GROUP DETAILS

13 — **WEEK 1 DISCUSSION**
- 16 — Devotion - Day 1
- 18 — Devotion - Day 2
- 20 — Devotion - Day 3
- 22 — Devotion - Day 4
- 24 — Devotion - Day 5

27 — **WEEK 2 DISCUSSION**
- 30 — Devotion - Day 1
- 32 — Devotion - Day 2
- 34 — Devotion - Day 3
- 36 — Devotion - Day 4
- 38 — Devotion - Day 5

41 — **WEEK 3 DISCUSSION**
- 44 — Devotion - Day 1
- 46 — Devotion - Day 2
- 48 — Devotion - Day 3
- 50 — Devotion - Day 4
- 52 — Devotion - Day 5

55 — **WEEK 4 DISCUSSION**
- 58 — Devotion - Day 1
- 60 — Devotion - Day 2
- 62 — Devotion - Day 3
- 64 — Devotion - Day 4
- 66 — Devotion - Day 5

69 — **WEEK 5 DISCUSSION**
- 72 — Devotion - Day 1
- 74 — Devotion - Day 2
- 76 — Devotion - Day 3
- 78 — Devotion - Day 4
- 80 — Devotion - Day 5

83 — **WEEK 6 DISCUSSION**
- 86 — Devotion - Day 1
- 88 — Devotion - Day 2
- 90 — Devotion - Day 3
- 92 — Devotion - Day 4
- 94 — Devotion - Day 5

WELCOME TO

Everyone wants to live the good life, but everyone has a different idea about how to get it. And we all have different ideas about what the good life actually is. Is it something you can only have if you're wealthy and retired or young and healthy? Many of us wrestle with this question as we hope to live the good life ourselves!

Jesus gives us an idea of where the good life comes from. In The Message translation of John 10:10, Jesus says: "A thief is only there to steal and kill and destroy. I came so they can have real and eternal life, more and better life than they ever dreamed of."

In this series, we give you a blueprint for how to live the Good Life – a life that is real, eternal and better than you ever dreamed of. The study is best done in community where you can watch and interact with the teachings together, discuss your devotional readings and pray for one another each week.

We pray God's blessing on you as you go through this journey. It is our hope that this series will help you find the Good Life – the life God created you to live.

HOW TO CREATE A SMALL GROUP

You don't have to be an expert in the Bible or have a special degree, a great teaching ability or prior small group experience. If you can do these four things, you will make a great small group **HOST**.

Have a heart for people.

Open your home (or provide another space) and invite a group of friends to join you.

Serve them a snack. Ask others to help after the first week.

Turn on the video. The video session will provide all of the teaching.

All of the discussion questions and outlines are included in this study guide. Just follow along. There's no experience needed so just enjoy the journey.

HOW TO GET THE MOST FROM THIS STUDY

1. Regularly attend the weekend services especially if using this study with the Good Life Sermon Series.

2. Spend 10 minutes a day engaging with the Daily Devotional. There are five for each week of the study. This gives you two extra days a week to reflect on what God has been doing through the Good Life study.

3. Regularly attend your small group. This will help you grow in your relationships with others as well as learn from the video teaching and the group discussion.

4. Pray for the people in your group throughout the week.

STRUCTURE OF A TYPICAL GROUP MEETING

Social time (15 minutes): This is a great time to serve coffee and snacks!

Icebreaker (10-15 minutes): Have each person say their name and respond to the icebreaker question.

Watch the Video (20-25 minutes)

Time of Discussion (45 minutes): The questions are provided. You don't need to get through them all – use them as a guide.

Ministry Time (15-20 minutes): Break up in smaller (usually single gender) groups and pray for one another.

LEADER RESOURCES

You will find many short, helpful training videos for new and experienced **HOST**s at **vcsmallgroups.org**.

Feel free to access these videos any time and come back to them as you have more questions.

TIPS FOR A GREAT SMALL GROUP

Being in a small group can be scary. Most people aren't comfortable sharing what they're going through with others. We've been hurt by people close to us so we try to keep our issues to ourselves and get through. Yet one of the biggest keys to living the Good Life is having a healthy group of friends who you are doing life with – a healthy small group. How do we create a great small group? Here are six tips.

1. Be friendly and be yourself. God wants to use you in your group through your unique gifts, personality and experiences. So be the real you with your strengths and weaknesses – don't try to be anyone else!

2. Silence is okay! When a question is asked, don't feel like you need to be the first person to jump in with an answer. Be aware of those who are quieter and give them an opportunity to share.

3. Pray for the other members of your group throughout the week. There is a roster in the back of each book where you can write the name and information of each group member so that you can be praying for them during the week.

4. Share responsibility for your group. You may have signed up to be the HOST, but each person can play a part. Some may want to help with the snack, while others might want to help lead discussion or even lead a time of worship before the meeting. Try to find a way that each person can play a role.

5. Don't worry about finishing all the questions. What's most important is that you connect as a group to see what God is doing in each of your lives and how you can support each other through life's ups and downs.

6. Have a meeting every week. Even if most of your group can't make it, God loves to work even when only a few people can come.

SMALL GROUP ROSTER

NAME	PHONE #	EMAIL

SMALL GROUP CALENDAR

Healthy groups share responsibilities and group ownership. It might take some time for this to develop, but shared ownership ensures that responsibility for the group doesn't fall to one person. Complete this calendar at your first or second meeting. Planning ahead will increase attendance and shared ownership.

DATE	LESSON	LOCATION	HOST	SNACK/MEAL
	1			
	2			
	3			
	4			
	5			
	6			

SMALL GROUP DISCUSSION GUIDE

" *THE GOOD LIFE IS LIVING THE LIFE GOD CREATED YOU TO LIVE.*

THE GOOD LIFE

ICEBREAKER

Share something you've done or experienced that really felt like you were living the good life – something fun or adventurous.

WATCH THE VIDEO

TEACHING OUTLINE

I. Common pictures of the Good Life

    A. Embrace every experience.

    B. Money and an attractive partner.

    C. Succeeding at my job.

    D. The wealthier you are the _____ you are.

II. The myth of these pictures leading to the Good Life

    A. The super-wealthy are not happier than the average American.

    B. The children of the super-wealthy have _____ outcomes than the average child.

    C. For men and women alike, the optimal number of sexual partners to achieve happiness and satisfaction is _____.

III. Jesus is the model for living the Good Life

    A. Jesus lived a life of _____. He lived the most liberated life that anyone ever lived.

        1. Jesus was free from regret.

        2. Jesus was free of guilt.

    B. Jesus turned into what _____ created him to be and to do.

BLANKS: *happier, worse, one, freedom, God*

DISCUSSION QUESTIONS

1. Do you agree with Rich that many people believe the good life consists of wealth and materials? Do you feel like the good life is only achieved if you can have a comfortable life – like afford healthcare or schooling for your kids? Why or why not?

2. Can you recall a time when you felt like all would be right with the world if only this one thing would happen? What are some things we might say stand between us and "the good life"?

JOHN 10:10: THE MESSAGE TRANSLATION SAYS:

"A thief is only there to steal and kill and destroy. I came so they can have real and eternal life, more and better life than they ever dreamed of."

3. Jesus talks about a "thief" that comes to steal, kill and destroy. When looking at our culture today, do you see what Jesus was talking about? If so, what are some examples?

4. What are some of the contributing factors to your worst days? Do you ever feel like there is someone actively rooting against you? Share your experience.

5. Rich says that to have the good life – a "real and better life than you ever dreamed of" – we need a good model to live by. He says that we are all imitators. Do you agree with him? Why or why not?

   What are some of your models for life?

6. In what ways would you like to follow a model like Jesus of Nazareth?

   What things about Jesus seem most difficult to imitate? What about your life right now would change if you started to imitate Christ in that area?

MINISTRY TIME

Ministry time is what we in the Vineyard call our prayer time for the group. It's really important that we not only discuss information – we also need to make space for God to meet with us personally. Each week, we'll have some simple directions for you to engage with God together as a group.

Take a few minutes to wait in silence. Don't rush this time! You might even want to set a timer to make sure you allow enough time. Silence can feel awkward, but it is important to make space for God to meet us. Just pray a simple prayer that invites God to come and be with you to begin this time.

After the time of silence, pray in at least one of these directions:

- Pray that God would be part of this group for the next six weeks and help you form as a community.
- Pray for God's blessing of the Good Life on the people in the group.
- Pray for a softness to Jesus as you go through this next six weeks together.
- Invite Jesus to be the model for each person in your group.

NOTES

Devotions
PSALM 23:1-2

1 The LORD is my shepherd, I lack nothing. 2 He makes me lie down in green pastures, he leads me beside quiet waters.

These are the opening lines to one of the most famous psalms from the Bible. Most people think King David of Israel wrote it. If anyone could claim to have the good life, you would think it would be a king. He had all the power and could seemingly have anything he wanted. But in this well-known psalm, King David describes himself as a sheep and God as his shepherd. This might be surprising, but the Bible often describes God as a shepherd. In John 10, Jesus actually calls himself "the good shepherd."

So what is it about God that makes him like a shepherd? And why does the Bible use this imagery so often? It's because God cares for us like a shepherd cares for his sheep. Since sheep are virtually helpless on their own, it's the shepherd who provides everything for them: food, water, safety and guidance. This is what King David had experienced from God and why he wrote this psalm. Even though the Bible tells us that every good thing comes from God (James 1:17), it's easy to believe that we are solely responsible for every good thing in our life, especially if you're the king. Not many of us like to feel helpless, but the reality is that we all have needs that we can't meet on our own.

In verse 2, David says, "He leads me beside quiet waters." When we are in need, one of the best things we can do is find a quiet place to spend time with God. Unfortunately, it's all too easy to become anxious and impatient instead. Struggling to trust God when we have needs, we often take matters into our own hands. But God really is a good Shepherd who loves to give us good things! So we find a quiet place and tell God what we need and ask him for his provision, protection and guidance.

Take a moment to read these verses again, out loud. Consider the ways God has provided, guided and protected you. Write these down in the Notes section. In times when following Jesus feels like anything but "the good life," you can look back and reflect on this list.

DIG DEEPER

Read all of Psalm 23 and continue to meditate on God as your shepherd – the one who guides you through all the ups and downs of life. How does this type of relationship with God allow you to experience "the good life" that he created you to live?

NOTES

Devotions
JOHN 15:4-5

4 Remain in me, as I also remain in you. No branch can bear fruit by itself; it must remain in the vine. Neither can you bear fruit unless you remain in me. 5 I am the vine; you are the branches. If you remain in me and I in you, you will bear much fruit; apart from me you can do nothing.

Yesterday, we reflected on God as a shepherd. Today, in these words of Jesus, we read of a different metaphor: he is the vine and we are the branches. Like a vine, Jesus is the source of your life and he holds together all its many parts: your career, your marriage, your family, your finances, your friendships, etc. As branches, our job is to stay connected to the vine so that we can produce "fruit" such as love, joy, peace and patience (Galatians 5:22-23).

"No branch can bear fruit by itself… apart from me you can do nothing." These were bold words for Jesus to say to his disciples, and to us today. There is no single thing we can accomplish outside of being connected to Jesus. The amazing thing is that he wants to always be connected with us and to help us when we're in need!

Spend 1-2 minutes quietly considering some ways you can "remain" in Jesus and bear good fruit: read the Bible several days a week, join a small group, take time each day to pray or regularly serve someone in need. Which of these ideas do you feel led to try out? Ask God to help you in this pursuit. No matter where you are on your journey with God, this would be a good exercise to do on a regular basis, as remaining in Jesus is essential for living "the good life," the one God created you to live.

DIG DEEPER

Read John 15:1-8 and spend some more time thinking about what it means to be connected to Jesus and what it specifically looks like to bear spiritual fruit.

NOTES

WEEK 1 DAY 3

Devotions
MATTHEW 4:1-4

1 Then Jesus was led by the Spirit into the wilderness to be tempted by the devil. 2 After fasting forty days and forty nights, he was hungry. 3 The tempter came to him and said, "If you are the Son of God, tell these stones to become bread." 4 Jesus answered, "It is written: 'Man shall not live on bread alone, but on every word that comes from the mouth of God.'"

Oxygen, water, food and shelter are essential for life. Beyond these absolute necessities though, three things are essential to experience the good life, the life God created you to live. First, we look at the life of Jesus, the only person who perfectly modeled the good life. That's the reason we pay such close attention to what he said and did in the Bible and seek to model our lives after his. Second, we regularly connect with Christians in settings such as a small group to help us better live out the good life that Jesus shows us. This will lead us to the third thing, which is living for the purpose for which God created you; this is what Jesus did and what he calls us to do also.

In these verses, Jesus, at the end of a 40-day fast, says to the devil, "Man shall not live on bread alone, but on every word that comes from the mouth of God." Jesus is saying that when we are in crisis, we can draw strength from the word of God. As we face things like the death of a loved one, chronic illness, job loss, etc., we should turn to the Bible because it contains the word of God, something that will bring us comfort and life during hard times.

Now, consider what Jesus isn't saying here, or anywhere in the Bible. He never claimed piles of money, lots of sex partners and a fancy house are essential for "the good life." Jesus lacked all of these things, and after 40 days of no food, he was still able to resist the temptation of the devil. Meanwhile, we often feel insecure when our bellies aren't full or when we don't have an abundance of material things. We have a misguided view of what's needed for "the good life."

Remember that Jesus said we live on every word of God. We find his words in the Bible, and we can even hear him speak when we pray. **Is reading the Bible or praying a challenge for you? If so, how do you think you can overcome the challenge so you are reading God's word and praying on a regular basis? Consider asking a friend to join you in this pursuit.** When you live on God's word, you begin living "the good life," the one he created you to live.

DIG DEEPER

Read Matthew 4:1-11. Imagine Jesus knowing very little scripture during this time of temptation. How might things have gone differently? Do you think greater knowledge of Jesus, via more frequent Bible reading, can help you during seasons of stress and temptation?

NOTES

WEEK 1 DAY 4 — Devotions
JOHN 16:33

33 "I have told you these things, so that in me you may have peace. In this world you will have trouble. But take heart! I have overcome the world."

Let's examine today's passage sentence by sentence. First, Jesus says, "I have told you these things, so that in me you may have peace." Jesus can tell you many things. Some of his words will bring you joy, some will confuse you, and some will initially scare you. Reading his words throughout the gospels is quite the emotional experience. Ultimately though, he promises us that we will find peace in him. He wants to fill every part of our lives with his peace – our bodies, our minds, our hearts, our relationships, etc.

Next, Jesus says, "In this world you will have trouble." Of all the truths proclaimed by Jesus, this statement probably rings most true for everyone – both those who follow Jesus and those who do not. Jesus doesn't avoid the truth that life can be tough, but as we read on we see he still promises that we can have the good life, the abundant life!

"But take heart!" Jesus likely raised his voice and gestured with his hands to make this point. Picture Jesus looking you in the eye and saying these words to you. To obey his command to "take heart" means that you place your hope in God, who will provide you with everything you need for "the good life." It also means current hardships pale in comparison to eternity with Jesus. **How can you become someone who is known to "take heart"? How can you help others to do the same?**

This verse concludes with these incredibly bold words: "I have overcome the world." Jesus is bigger than your loneliness, your heartbreak, your failures, your grief, your mistakes, your trauma and your disease. **Ask God to transform your perspective on what it really means to live "the good life" and that it would fill you with hope whenever you face hardship.**

DIG DEEPER

Read John 16:16-33 and return again to what Jesus said in John 10:10: "The thief comes only to steal and kill and destroy; I have come that they may have life, and have it to the full." How do these words relate to what he says here in John 16? After reading these verses, what is one thing you will begin to do differently?

22 *the Good Life*

NOTES

WEEK 1 DAY 5 — Devotions
2 CORINTHIANS 5:17

17 Therefore, if anyone is in Christ, the new creation has come: The old has gone, the new is here!

What an incredible promise: the old has gone and the new has come! Think about how being "in Christ" is what makes this possible. It's what transforms and improves your private life: your thoughts, your alone time, your home life, your leisure time, your finances, your time spent on the Internet, etc. It impacts your public life: your career, your time at school, your friendships, your driving habits, your time at church, etc.

But what if you aren't sure whether you are actually in "in Christ"? Perhaps you've never received Jesus' forgiveness or thought about whether he is worth following. Or maybe you've been on a slow journey away from him for quite some time. Perhaps you're in the midst of a really horrible day or week and Jesus feels far, far away. No matter where you are, the invitation to receive his new creation is always there.

Accepting this invitation will look different from person to person, but the access point is the same: prayer. Here are some things you may want to say to God: tell him you're sorry for trying to do life apart from Jesus. Ask for mercy and healing from your hurts and habits. Pray that your faith would grow and that your life would exude fruit such as love, joy, kindness and self-control. Ask God to usher you into "the good life," to spark in you a willingness to receive the life he created you to live. **Talk to God about where you are now and tell him where you want to be. Where do you want the "new" to replace the "old"? Who else in your life do you sense is disconnected from Jesus? Pray for them as well, that God would bring this new creation into their lives, too.**

DIG DEEPER

Read 2 Corinthians 5:16-21. Note Paul's frequent mentions of reconciliation. One of the aspects of being reconciled to God means that we are now called his friend. How does this friendship impact your life?

NOTES

SMALL GROUP DISCUSSION GUIDE

> *WHEN WE LIVE OUT OUR CALLING, WE WILL FIND A GENUINE SENSE OF FULFILLMENT.*

THE GOOD LIFE: LIVING A LIFE OF CALLING

ICEBREAKER

What was your first job or what was a job you had that was out-of-the-ordinary?

WATCH THE VIDEO

TEACHING OUTLINE

I. Common ways to search for the purpose and meaning of your life

    A. Having a multitude of pleasurable experiences.

    B. Finding meaning in past hurts or _____.

    C. Finding meaning and purpose only through our jobs is _____.

    D. Looking inside of yourself.

II. Finding God's purpose and meaning for your life

    A. The Good Life is a response to the _____ of God.

        1. The first call is to belong to God.

        2. The second call is to belong to God's family.

    B. We become "salt" and "light" in the world by becoming the _____ _____ of ourselves that God intended us to be.

BLANKS: *theraputism, workaholism, call, best version*

DISCUSSION QUESTIONS

1. What internal or external pressures push people into being "workaholics"? Why do you think there is so much pressure to find fulfillment in work and performance in our culture?

2. What is your experience of work or performance? Do your passions and work line up? Do you find yourself consumed by work or bored and disconnected?

3. Rich talked about the need for us to belong to a community as we figure out what we are made for – "our calling." Can you remember a time when you didn't feel like you belonged to a community – where you felt you were on the outside looking in? Can you name some factors that made you feel that way?

   Now can you think of a time when you felt you really belonged to a community? What were the key elements that made you feel a part of that group?

READ MATTHEW 5:13-16

5. Jesus uses the images of salt and light. Salt was used in the ancient world to preserve food as well as a seasoning for food. Why do you think Jesus chose these images to explain to his followers how to be on this earth?

   How would it look to be "salt" or "light" in this world according to Jesus?

6. Spend a few minutes doing Rich's exercise:

   Fill in the blank, "When God made me, he made me like this: _____. This is when I feel God's pleasure – this is when I feel truly right with the world when I am doing this."

   Share with the group what you filled in. If you need help thinking through this question, think of Rich's other question: What is the central drive in your life that motivates you to do your particular job, or your particular acts of service?

MINISTRY TIME

This week do some personal prayer. Ask God to bless his calling on each person's life. If you have a large group, break down in groups of two or three to pray for each other.

An example prayer:

"Jesus, would you please bless _____? Would you reveal in a deeper and fuller way how you have made them?"

NOTES

WEEK 2 / DAY 1

Devotions
JOHN 6:38

38 For I have come down from heaven not to do my will but to do the will of him who sent me.

On any given day, we have many things to accomplish; we always seem to be on the go. We hope to slow down and connect with God and others, but we often don't succeed in walking out this fine balance. In the chaos of day-to-day life, you may question whether you're actually doing what you sense you've been called to do. The word or phrase that describes the reality of your life may be quite different than what you want it to be about. This disconnect can be quite frustrating. Why does it happen? What's the solution?

Intentionally or not, we model our lives after someone. This person influences what we do on a daily basis, the goals we set, the things we choose to leave undone, etc.

Perhaps it's a parent, a teacher, a friend, a sibling or even a famous person. **Take a moment to consider people you admire and how they influence your life.**

Now let's take a look at how admiration for Jesus and allowing his example to guide you is one of the chief ways to live the good life, the one God created you to live. Jesus did not have his own personal agenda. His mission was to do the will of God. He was certain this was what he was called to do. We should do what Jesus did; we should actively seek to do God's will in any and all situations. This will lead us into the good life. **Closely examine every area of your life: your job, your relationships, your finances, etc. Invite God into any areas you've shut him out of. Surrender your agenda to him and ask what he is calling you to do instead.**

DIG DEEPER

Read John 6:35-40 to get a better picture of what doing God's will looked like in the life of Jesus. He invested everything in giving life to the full to his followers. What do you want to say to Jesus about this tremendous life of love? What does it inspire you to do?

NOTES

WEEK 2 DAY 2 — Devotions
MATTHEW 9:9

9 As Jesus went on from there, he saw a man named Matthew sitting at the tax collector's booth. "Follow me," he told him, and Matthew got up and followed him.

Someone knocks on your door; you open it. Your telephone rings; you answer it. You receive an invitation to a party; you RSVP. Or not. Perhaps the call comes at a really inconvenient time. Your kid is having a meltdown or you have a looming work deadline or you're in the middle of a Netflix binge. Maybe you are a fierce introvert and you're particularly burnt out on people right now. Maybe you're avoiding the specific person who's calling you.

In this verse from the gospel of Matthew, we find a man who immediately dropped everything to follow Jesus. Why? Perhaps Matthew was an extroverted people pleaser. Despite having a secure and prosperous job, maybe he found something deeply lacking about his life; so he decided to give Jesus a try. Or perhaps there was something so lovely and captivating about Jesus that there was no way he could ignore the call. Maybe it's all of the above. Regardless, he responded so quickly that it's noteworthy, perhaps even unsettling.

Today, what do you sense Jesus calling you toward? Ask God this question then spend three minutes in silence, listening for his voice. This may feel uncomfortable, especially if you've never done this before. Or maybe you already sense his call but you've chosen to avoid answering as of late. Nonetheless, trust that the Lord will meet you in the discomfort. Perhaps he wants you to let him into a certain area of your life, one you normally try to hide from him. Maybe he is calling you to reach out to someone in need or is revealing some specific ways for you to be a more loving spouse. **Both in the short-term and the long-term, how is he calling you to enter into the good life he created you to live? Write down whatever you sense God speaking and pray you would be faithful to respond to his call. This week, share this list with your small group.**

DIG DEEPER

Read Matthew 9:9-13. Matthew experienced a reputation downgrade when he started following Jesus. Some of the things God calls you to do require sacrifice and loss. Are you ready for this? Think about how time spent praying, reading the Bible, attending a small group, etc., will help you through those seasons when the drawbacks of answering Jesus' call are pronounced or prolonged.

NOTES

WEEK 2 DAY 3 — Devotions
LUKE 10:2-3

2 He told them, "The harvest is plentiful, but the workers are few. Ask the Lord of the harvest, therefore, to send out workers into his harvest field. 3 Go! I am sending you out like lambs among wolves."

God calls each of his followers to proclaim the Good News of Jesus to the world – to point everyone toward his love. How this relates to harvesting crops from a field may seem puzzling to us but it surely resonated with the farmers of Jesus' day: harvesting while the fields were ripe and plentiful was an urgent matter; otherwise the crops would be lost. This means we should not let opportunities to communicate God's love to the world pass us by. We must go out into the field and do this work we sense God calling us to do. However, the landscape of today's spiritual harvest field is treacherous. The world is often not a welcoming place for Christians. No wonder Jesus said we are "like lambs among wolves" whenever he sends us out. Feeling vulnerable and defenseless is warranted and not uncommon.

A friend may be interested in spirituality, but he is skeptical of "organized religion." When the subject of Christianity comes up at a family gathering, your cousin, a vocal atheist, is seated across from you at the table. Your teen finds your guidelines for curfew, screen time and relationships unreasonable and punishing, so she shuts you out entirely. These are the harvest fields of your life, and you are the worker. What does this mean? According to Jesus' words in verse 3, God may be asking you to invite these people to join you on the journey toward embracing the good life, the one he created us to live.

How does this make you feel? What work does God want you to do in the many harvest fields of your life: work, home, neighborhood, school, etc.? What are some specific ways you can point the people in all these places toward Jesus? Remember, Jesus knows this calling can be scary. He said we would feel like lambs, animals that are known for being afraid of everything. **Honestly offer your fears up to the Lord. What do you sense him speaking to your heart?**

DIG DEEPER

Read Luke 10:1-16. When it comes to the work of pointing people toward Jesus, how can you determine when God wants you to keep working where you are or when he wants you to move on to a new setting?

NOTES

WEEK 2 DAY 4

Devotions
GENESIS 12:4

4 So Abram went, as the LORD had told him; and Lot went with him. Abram was seventy-five years old when he set out from Harran.

We feel pressured to choose a major in college and stick with it. If you're not married by age 30, your mom and grandma attempt to fix you up with anyone and everyone. Notable geniuses such as Einstein and Descartes did their greatest work in their twenties. Overall, our culture tends to think that the significant things of life must happen at a young age and that the elderly don't do anything of importance. The Bible turns this thinking upside down. Here in Genesis we read that one of the most important callings of all time happened to someone when he was 75 years old. Wow!

If for whatever reason you think you don't qualify as someone God would call, you're wrong. Abram didn't say to God, "Thanks, but I'll pass. I'm too old." Instead, in his old age, "Abram went, as the Lord had told him." Abram is the type of person who never stops asking God questions like, "What is the good life you've created me to live?" and, "Jesus, what's next?"

When God calls people, he calls anyone and everyone. No one gets left out. You're not too old, too young, too poor or too rich. Your marital status, nationality, level of education, gender or ethnicity will never exclude you from God's call into something amazing. Neither your past, nor your family background, nor your personality will keep God from calling you toward new adventures, great challenges and many opportunities to experience the good life he intends for you.

Take several minutes to write down your passions and talents, all those things that move your heart. Pray, asking God to illuminate some of the ideas and to give you an action plan to accompany them. What is the first step you will take to begin walking out these callings? As these adventures unfold, remember that God will be pleased with you because he will recognize that you're living the good life, the one he created you to live. **How does this make you feel?**

DIG DEEPER

Read Genesis 12:1-9. This call is big, not just for Abram but for the whole world. Through Abram, God would create a great nation that would bless all people on earth. Not everything God calls you to do will be this monumental. How can you become more sensitive to his call in the smaller, day-to-day things?

NOTES

Week 2, Day 5 — Devotions
EPHESIANS 4:1

1 As a prisoner for the Lord, then, I urge you to live a life worthy of the calling you have received.

As we've learned this week, a sense of calling is an exciting, sometimes scary aspect of following Jesus. Following God's calling and committing to it for the long haul require a foundation of complete dedication to Jesus. We can't be in it simply to get noticed or to feel important! We need all of Jesus in all areas of our lives. Otherwise, we will not please God; we will crash and burn.

Paul is urging his audience to "live a life worthy of the calling you have received." Let's say a friend or family member you don't see much is suddenly on your mind a lot, but you don't know why. Or maybe you have a dream about the person. Thinking this may be God asking you to reach out to the person, you start hanging out with him more often, you pray for him, and you take time to really listen to everything he shares with you about his life. You sense a closeness developing, and you even have a chance to talk to him about following Jesus. But you feel some hesitation because you know you've got things in your own life that aren't pleasing to God. Maybe every time you have a chance to share the good life you have in Jesus, you don't because you feel like a hypocrite. This feeling of inconsistency could be an invitation from God to start living in more freedom.

Ask God to reveal one place in your life where your talk doesn't line up with your walk. What do you sense him speaking? Also ask him to give you one idea to free you from this struggle. How will you begin to walk this out? Perhaps you could share this struggle with a friend or someone from your small group. Remember, you don't have to try to make these changes on your own; every good gift comes from God, and that includes his ability to transform each aspect of your life so that you are indeed living the life he created you to live.

DIG DEEPER

Read Ephesians 4:1-16 and think some more about how pursuing spiritual maturity will lead you toward a life that is "worthy of the calling you have received." What are some specific ways to do this?

NOTES

SMALL GROUP DISCUSSION GUIDE

> *"EVENTUALLY, EVERYONE AROUND YOU WILL SEE WHAT YOU ARE MADE OF. LIVING A GOOD LIFE – THE LIFE GOD CREATED YOU TO LIVE – COMES FROM THE INSIDE OUT.*

THE GOOD LIFE: LIVING A LIFE OF CHARACTER

ICEBREAKER

Who is one of the most inspiring or significant people in your life? What makes them inspirational to you?

WATCH THE VIDEO

TEACHING OUTLINE

I. The Personality Ethic of modern culture

    A. Based on personality traits.

        1. Positive mental attitude.

        2. Can-do attitude.

    B. Based on particular _____ skills.

        1. Influence through engagement.

        2. Influence through how we're perceived.

II. The Character Ethic of Jesus

    A. Based on a life of _____.

    B. Based on choosing the right _____ to follow.

        1. Observing and doing what the model does.

        2. Christians assert there is no better model than Jesus.

    C. Based in community.

        1. Our close friends will help determine who we become.

        2. People need others to point out their weaknesses.

    D. Based in suffering.

        1. Helps us recognize our _____.

        2. Helps us live a life of gratitude.

BLANKS: *social, integrity, model, limitations*

DISCUSSION QUESTIONS

A reminder to Hosts: don't feel like you need to do every question – the point is not to cover everything. Rather, see where God is leading the group. Allow the group to spend more time on questions that are creating good discussion or skip others that don't seem relative.

1. Have you taken a personality test? What are the things that you like about your character or personality? What are things you wish you could change?

READ ROMANS 7:15-25

2. Paul, an early missionary and pastor of the church, wrote to a group of followers in Rome about his own experience of following Jesus. Can you summarize what Paul is saying about the "war within him" in your own words?

3. Becoming a person with good character can be really challenging. The Message version of verse 16 says:

   "What I don't understand about myself is that I decide one way, but then I act another, doing things I absolutely despise."

   Do you resonate with Paul? Do you ever feel at war with yourself? Why do you think this is a challenge?

   Would a few of you talk about an instance when you intended to do something right and you chose to do something wrong instead? Or a time when you chose to do right even though the decision was unpopular with those around you?

   Rich suggests three things that God uses to develop good character and bring peace to the war within us that Paul talks about: Having the right models, being in community and suffering.

4. Who or what most influences the way you think, feel or act? Is there a book or movie that has had a particularly influential role in the way you imagine things? Do your friends' tastes and opinions generally match or even inform your own?

5. Do you agree that community allows you to form character? Have you been a part of a community that has truly shaped who you are? Would you be willing to share?

6. Do you think it is possible to see suffering used for good? How so?
   Share a time when you went through deep pain or difficulty that developed your character.

MINISTRY TIME

Pray all together or break down in smaller groups. Start by inviting God's presence and spending a few minutes in silence to allow God to guide the group. Recall what you discussed, especially moments when you felt a pull at your heart or a heightening of emotions when someone shared something. These are likely times when God was speaking to your group. Here are some ideas for directions to pray:

- Pray for the ability to see the areas in life where your model is not bringing you life. Ask God for help to follow Jesus as a model.

- Pray for your group to form as a meaningful community that really helps each other discover what God created you for.

- Pray for those in the group who are experiencing suffering. Pray that God would be present and meet them in this season.

NOTES

WEEK 3 DAY 1 — Devotions

1 SAMUEL 16:7

7 But the LORD said to Samuel, "Do not consider his appearance or his height, for I have rejected him. The LORD does not look at the things people look at. People look at the outward appearance, but the LORD looks at the heart."

Our culture breeds obsession about things that ultimately don't matter. The inner monologue of Americans sounds like this: "I must be the perfect weight. Going to that college is akin to social suicide. My clothing must be name brand and on trend. I'd give just about anything to have perfectly sculpted abs. I can't live in that neighborhood; what would people say about me? I would never drive that car. This tooth whitener is going to change my life! I've been single for so long; people must think I'm such a loser." These concerns have nothing at all to do with your heart or with what matters most to God. And yet they continue to plague our thoughts.

When he assesses people, God does not look at appearance; he's not looking at the things people look at. God wants us to do the same – to disregard looks and social status when we evaluate people. How amazing would it be if we could focus on those things that express someone's character and heart instead?

Spend some time in prayer today asking God about your character. What encouragement does God have to offer you? In what ways does he want to help you look more like him? Also, spend some time thinking about people in your life whose heart and character look like Jesus. What could you say to them to acknowledge that? How do they inspire you to be more like Jesus?

DIG DEEPER

Read 1 Samuel 16:1-13. How might Samuel's reliance on God in choosing David as king apply to your own life? Perhaps you are interviewing candidates for a job, or maybe you are considering dating someone. What do we miss out on if we concentrate solely on the outward appearance of others? What do we gain by looking deeper?

NOTES

WEEK 3 DAY 2 — Devotions
MATTHEW 25:21

21 "His master replied, 'Well done, good and faithful servant! You have been faithful with a few things; I will put you in charge of many things. Come and share your master's happiness!'"

People with good character are faithful in the "little things." They RSVP to invitations, drive courteously, abstain from social media and personal texts while at work and speak well of their spouses. They also do things like regularly read the Bible and pray, host a small group and show up at church even when they don't feel like it. Faithfulness in the little things spans all areas of life, sacred and secular.

In this verse from a parable, which is a simple story used to communicate spiritual truth, a master entrusted his servant with something small but valuable. Maybe God has placed something similar in your care. Perhaps you lead or host a small group. Maybe you are a stay-at-home parent to your small children or you care for an elderly relative. As you carry out these responsibilities, God is likely proclaiming to you, "Well done, good and faithful servant!"

Greater responsibility often follows this type of faithfulness. If you are faithfully hosting a small group, your leader may ask you to go through leadership training so that you can soon start your own group. If you provide consistent, compassionate care to your aging mother, God may ask you to gather a group of volunteers at church to provide eldercare to isolated senior citizens in your community. Faithfulness in the "little things" makes way for big assignments from God.

The final sentence of this verse is, "Come and share your master's happiness!" According the original language of Aramaic, "joy" or "festival" may be a better translation than "happiness." Faithfully completing God-given assignments ushers us toward joy, toward "the good life." Moreover, desiring more of God's intentions for us is evidence of good character. **What is one thing you think God has entrusted to you? Ask God that you would faithfully care for that thing, and whenever you notice an increase in responsibility, say thank you to God for getting to share in his joy.**

DIG DEEPER

Read the entire parable in Matthew 25:14-30. In verse 25, the "wicked servant" says, "So I was afraid…" Consider whether fear interferes with your ability to be faithful to whatever God entrusts to you. What fears can you hand off to God right now, and what fears can you invite God to settle over this season?

NOTES

WEEK 3 DAY 3 — Devotions
ACTS 5:3-4

3 Then Peter said, "Ananias, how is it that Satan has so filled your heart that you have lied to the Holy Spirit and have kept for yourself some of the money you received for the land? 4 Didn't it belong to you before it was sold? And after it was sold, wasn't the money at your disposal? What made you think of doing such a thing? You have not lied just to human beings but to God."

Telling the truth is a hallmark of a life of character. Truth-tellers are trustworthy. People feel safe when they're around someone who won't lie to them. And yet, honesty is neither widely practiced nor explicitly valued. There are so many opportunities to lie. We gloss over unsavory details about ourselves. Everyone "stretches the truth." When we are deceitful or when we hurt someone, we rarely tell on ourselves; if we confess, we don't do so until we're caught. We fear conflict with others, so we lie. In fact, fear of all sorts of things is at the root of every single lie we tell. This is a sad state of affairs, but the good news is that God can help us overcome whatever motivates us to lie. This way, we can live lives that are free from the anxiety and fear that comes from hiding and stretching the truth.

It cannot be overstated: honesty with yourself, with God and with others is essential for living a life of character. When you lie, it is impossible to fully live the good life: the one God created you to live. In this text from Acts, we read about a time when the Apostle Peter accused a man named Ananias of being anything but honest. He insists, "Satan has so filled" Ananias' heart that he has "lied to the Holy Spirit" and that he has "not lied just to human beings but to God." Wow. These are not light charges.

Do you agree with the phrase, "the truth will set you free"? How do you think telling the truth could make a person free? Do you have a lie or deception in your life that you know you should confess? Invite God into this situation and make a plan to take one step toward honesty. Remember, he is with you and wants to provide you with everything you need to live the good life, the one he created you to live, and that includes enough bravery to be honest.

DIG DEEPER

Read Acts 5:1-11. This is one of the most intense stories in the Bible. After Ananias and Sapphira lied to God and to his church, they died. Share your reaction to this story with God. What response do you sense from him?

NOTES

Devotions
MATTHEW 26:73-75

73 After a little while, those standing there went up to Peter and said, "Surely you are one of them; your accent gives you away." 74 Then he began to call down curses, and he swore to them, "I don't know the man!" Immediately a rooster crowed. 75 Then Peter remembered the word Jesus had spoken: "Before the rooster crows, you will disown me three times." And he went outside and wept bitterly.

Yesterday we examined poor character by looking at a time when Peter exposed someone in a lie. Today, in the gospel of Matthew the tables are turned on Peter: he is the liar. He lied out of fear to save his own skin. This was no ordinary time in Peter's life; Jesus was under arrest and his crucifixion was imminent. Followers of Jesus, like Peter, feared the same fate awaited them. Usually, when the heat is on, the ugly comes out. Maybe you shut down and isolate yourself from others. Maybe you go into a rage. Maybe you overeat. When you are squeezed, what comes out of you says a lot about your character.

But what about when the difficult moment subsides and you have time to consider your reaction? In this gospel passage we read, "Then Peter remembered the words Jesus had spoken..." he quickly and regrettably realized how much he screwed up. "He went outside and wept bitterly." Some of the most emotionally trying times in life are when we realize we've done something very egregious or harmful. We struggle with how to respond. Perhaps you refuse to admit it to others because you are ashamed and fear the conversation it will require. Maybe you drown the mistake in alcohol or a shopping spree. God invites us to a better life than that! He invites us to a good life where we can receive his love and be fully honest with him about our mistakes so that he can fill us with resolve to do the right thing going forward.

If your default is to do wrong instead of right when under pressure, take heart! If you fumble even further once you've realized the mistake, be encouraged! A life of character is a journey and Jesus is the source of all progress. In fact, in John 21, after Jesus is resurrected, he powerfully reinstates Peter, inviting him again into the good life, the one God created him to live. No mistake, no sin, no character flaw is outside the reach of God's great love and power. **Conclude by giving your failures over to God. In return, as a sign of openness to him, open your hands and receive God's love in all areas of your life.**

DIG DEEPER

Read Matthew 26:69-75. Picture yourself as a bystander. Imagine Peter's body language, his facial expressions and his tone of voice. What else is God revealing as you insert yourself into this story?

NOTES

WEEK 3 DAY 5 — Devotions
ROMANS 7:18-19

18 For I know that good itself does not dwell in me, that is, in my sinful nature. For I have the desire to do what is good, but I cannot carry it out. 19 For I do not do the good I want to do, but the evil I do not want to do – this I keep on doing.

This week we've taken a close look at a life of character. People with good character are known for their heart, not any outward markers; they are faithful in the little things; they tell the truth; and they do the right thing when under pressure. No one wakes up one day and suddenly starts perfectly embodying these things. They require incredibly hard work and lots of patience. It's tempting to frustratingly throw up your hands and ask, "Why even try?"

The Apostle Paul, in his letter to the Romans, appears to know exactly how we feel. His words here in chapter 7 are a bit of a tongue twister: I don't do what I want to do; I do what I don't want to do. Tongue twister or not, the words are true and powerful. Philosophers of all faiths call this moral helplessness, a condition that afflicts us all. Despite even the most admirable of beliefs, we often make bad decisions in the moment due to a lack of self-control. What we do does not always coincide with our core convictions. We are all hypocrites.

Again, you may be asking, "So why even try?" You're right; trying to overcome moral helplessness on your own is like bailing water out of a boat with a hole in it; you're still going to sink. Thankfully, we are never forced to figure out how to live the good life on our own. God gives us other people. Together, we can help each other to do what is good – to help each other make choices that align with the good life God created us to live. An ideal setting for this is a small group, an intentional community where you genuinely know, care for, and encourage one another. **Do you have this kind of meaningful community in your life? If not, what is one thing that is holding you back from it? Ask God to remove this barrier so that you can experience the good life alongside other people.**

DIG DEEPER

Read Romans 7:7-25 to get a bigger picture of Paul's struggle to do the right thing. Meditate on the truth that no matter how frustrated you are by your failures to do right or how trapped you feel by your sin, Jesus will rescue you. How does this make you feel? What do you want to say to God about it?

NOTES

SMALL GROUP DISCUSSION GUIDE

> *COMPASSION IS PART OF LIVING THE GOOD LIFE JESUS CAME TO GIVE US BECAUSE, IF THERE IS ONE QUALITY THAT JESUS MODELED ABOVE ALL ELSE, IT WOULD BE COMPASSION.*

THE GOOD LIFE: LIVING A LIFE OF COMPASSION

ICEBREAKER

When you watch the news or look out at the world today, what tugs at your heart? What situations or circumstances move you to compassion?

WATCH THE VIDEO

TEACHING OUTLINE

I. Compassion in the Bible

    A. Having mercy on someone.

    B. Caring for someone like a mother would her _____.

    C. Feeling for them in your emotions, your soul, your guts.

    D. Being willing to suffer with someone.

II. Perceived barriers to showing Compassion

    A. We believe we are too busy.

    B. We believe the problem is too complicated to fix.

    C. We believe that discussing something is the same as _____ something.

    D. We don't believe that we could be potential victims in need.

    E. We believe the _____ is too high.

III. Growing in Compassion

    A. Get close to people in _____.

    B. Start by partnering with your friends in community.

BLANKS: *newborn/child, doing, price, need*

DISCUSSION QUESTIONS

1. Do you know anyone who is a truly compassionate person? What are they like? How do they make you feel?

READ LUKE 10:25-37

2. When the man asks Jesus what he must do to inherit eternal life, what is the first thing that Jesus points him to do? (verse 26) Have you ever considered looking to the Bible for an answer when you need it? Why or why not?

3. In verse 29, what reason does the scripture give for the man asking Jesus: "Who is my neighbor?"? What kind of answer do you think he was expecting? What do you think he felt when he heard Jesus' story of the Samaritan as the answer?

4. Who do you have difficulty seeing as a "neighbor"? Why are they difficult to show compassion for?

5. Do you find it easier to talk about compassion rather than take action? What is one thing you could do together as a group to act in compassion?

MINISTRY TIME

Pray and ask God to speak to you about the ideas for action that were discussed as a group. Take a few minutes of silence and invite God to show you which idea he would like you to try. After waiting for God for a few minutes, discuss any impressions as a group and make a plan to do one thing this week together to act in compassion.

NOTES

WEEK 4 DAY 1 — Devotions

EXODUS 34:5-7

5 Then the LORD came down in the cloud and stood there with him and proclaimed his name, the LORD. 6 And he passed in front of Moses, proclaiming, "The LORD, the LORD, the compassionate and gracious God, slow to anger, abounding in love and faithfulness, 7 maintaining love to thousands, and forgiving wickedness, rebellion and sin."

A common misconception about the Old Testament is that it's just a bunch of strange and incredibly harsh rules about the Sabbath, food and sex created by a punitive God. In reality, it is rich with accounts of God's great compassion and mercy toward all people. The Bible tells us that God never changes, so it's not like he was a big bully in the Old Testament and nothing but peace, love and harmony in the New Testament. God didn't withhold his compassion prior to sending his son Jesus to Earth. Rather, he lavished it upon the world. He hung a rainbow in the sky after the great flood. He parted the Red Sea so that people could flee slavery and oppression. God showed his love to his people over and over again. An understanding of God's compassion across all of eternity and how it impacts us to our core are important components of living the good life he created us to live.

In this text from Exodus, Moses has an encounter with all-powerful and perfectly holy God. Imagine having a meeting with a world leader or *Fortune* 500 CEO. You may expect him to assert power and dominance, to brag about his wealth and influence, and to be merciless in his dealings with you. Not so with God. He could take this opportunity with Moses to punish or to boast about his power to bring harm, but he talks about his compassion, grace, patience, love and faithfulness instead. How amazing! If God didn't share these kindnesses, these components of his incredible love with us, his creation, we would have no hope of ever living the good life.

Take a moment to read this passage out loud. Then, make a list of all the ways God describes himself in verses 6-7. Write down some of the ways God reveals these attributes to you in your own life. What do you want to say to God about showing his compassion to you in these ways?

DIG DEEPER

Read Exodus 34:4-14. This is an excerpt of when Moses recorded the Ten Commandments for the second time. In verses 8-9, as Moses worshipped and prayed, we see he approached God as though he were compassionate. Do you view God as compassionate? Why or why not? Try writing down some of your thoughts as a prayer to God.

NOTES

WEEK 4 DAY 2

Devotions

MATTHEW 25:37-40

37 "Then the righteous will answer him, 'Lord, when did we see you hungry and feed you, or thirsty and give you something to drink? 38 When did we see you a stranger and invite you in, or needing clothes and clothe you? 39 When did we see you sick or in prison and go to visit you? 40 "The King will reply, 'Truly I tell you, whatever you did for one of the least of these brothers and sisters of mine, you did for me.'"

Hunger, thirst, poverty, illness and imprisonment existed in Jesus' day and they exist in our own. How do these problems manifest in today's complex world? Tonight, children in our own city will go to bed hungry. Around 783 million people across the globe do not have access to clean drinking water. Refugees flee their war-torn homes and escape to unfamiliar countries only to be turned away. More than one billion people in the world struggle to live on less than a dollar a day. Compared to those living in the Western world, children in developing countries and those living in poverty are up to 84 times more likely to die by the age of five. The United States has the highest prison population rate in the world. These injustices grieve the heart of God because he is a God of compassion. Moreover, Jesus tells us in this text from the gospel of Matthew, that when we show compassion toward someone by feeding the hungry, welcoming an immigrant, visiting a prisoner, etc., we are actually doing it for Jesus himself.

Notice how many times the "righteous" in this text ask, "Lord, when did we see..." Compassion first requires that we actually see problems around us – those people and places in need of mercy and love. But for many reasons, we often fail to do this: to see. We're too busy, the situation is too complicated, or maybe we don't want to be inconvenienced. The good news is that God wants to help us see these things so that they deeply move us toward compassion. You may be thinking to yourself, "Where do I start? There are way too many problems in the world; I'm overwhelmed. Surely I can't make a difference!" Start by asking God to open your eyes in the everyday of life. What hurts and injustices do you encounter, and what does God want you to do about them? God wants to make you sensitive to these things and inspire you with ideas to help remedy them. For example, you could start keeping some bags of non-perishable groceries in your trunk. The next time you see someone standing at the exit ramp holding a sign asking for help, rather than averting your gaze, give him a bag of those groceries.

Remember, Jesus wants us to see: to see injustices and to remedy them. When we encounter "the least," someone who is hungry, new to this country, sick, in prison or any combination of the above, God is likely asking us to stop, to see, to allow it to move us and to help. **What is just one way you can show compassion by seeing someone, the way Jesus talks about it in this Matthew text? Do it this week and share about the experience with your small group.**

DIG DEEPER

Read Matthew 25:31-46. Failure to care for the least among us has grave consequences. But what about the opposite problem: compassion fatigue? Consider whether you rely on your own finite resources instead of drawing from God whenever you serve others. Ask Jesus for his strength, love and grace to serve.

NOTES

WEEK 4 DAY 3 — Devotions — MATTHEW 14:14

14 When Jesus landed and saw a large crowd, he had compassion on them and healed their sick.

Two millennia ago, when the first followers of Jesus started spreading the news about the good life God was offering to all people, they visited Athens, Greece, a city with a very interesting vibe. Acts 17:34 sums it up quite well: "All the Athenians and the foreigners who lived there spent their time doing nothing but talking about and listening to the latest ideas." Sounds familiar, right? Especially in the current landscape of social media. Someone may not vote in an off-year election, but he will post a lot of political memes on Facebook. Your "decorating" Pinterest board may be full of lovely ideas, but all of the photos and artwork in the apartment you've lived in for over a year remain unhung. Thinking about something is completely different than doing something.

How does this relate to the life of compassion? In our culture, thinking about compassion happens a lot more than actually doing compassion. You scroll past endless political arguments on Facebook. You read newspaper editorials from different experts espousing all the best ways to solve the world's great injustices. Or maybe you've spent many a late night hanging out with friends debating solutions to societal ills. It's great to think deeply about problems in the world and it's helpful to hash them out with friends. These things can stir up compassion within your heart. But no amount of thinking or debating will nourish a hungry child or lead to racial reconciliation. Part of living the good life is not only having compassion in your heart and on your mind, but allowing it to overflow into your actions. Everything from speaking kindly to your young child when she is testing your patience to volunteering at a food pantry on a Saturday morning instead of sleeping in are times of moving from thinking about compassion to doing compassion.

Jesus, the perfect model for living the good life, didn't sit around debating the best way to care for the sick. In this single sentence from the gospel of Matthew, we see what he did instead: he healed the sick people in a large crowd. It is such a simple but powerful act. Step one: he had a compassionate thought. Step two: he did compassion. Throughout the gospels, we see Jesus do this time and time again. **Instead of simply feeling bad or hoping someone**

else figures it out, consider how you can follow Jesus' example: where might God be calling you to use compassion to help someone?

DIG DEEPER

Read Matthew 14:13-21. There are a few layers to Jesus' compassion in this text: he heals people because he has compassion on them and he wants to make sure they don't go hungry. Along with a friend or perhaps with your small group, make a plan to read and study Jesus' acts of compassion throughout the gospels.

NOTES

WEEK 4 DAY 4

Devotions
LUKE 6:35-36

35 But love your enemies, do good to them, and lend to them without expecting to get anything back. Then your reward will be great, and you will be children of the Most High, because he is kind to the ungrateful and wicked. 36 Be merciful, just as your Father is merciful.

An even exchange, like loving people who readily love you back, is not an act of compassion. Compassionate acts are not "fair." "Fairness" is not a core value in God's kingdom. Compassionate people don't ask, "What's in it for me?" In purely economic terms, living a good life of compassion doesn't make sense.

Christians and churches use the word "mercy" a lot, but many don't know what it actually means or how it relates to compassion. When you are merciful, as God calls us to be in this text, it means you make a decision to be kind and compassionate toward someone who is undeserving of such treatment. Even though she talks about you behind your back, you show kindness to your co-worker and cover a shift for her. Enduring years of unfair treatment by a family member, you still help him move on a freezing cold Saturday in January when you'd much rather be cozy in bed with a cup of coffee and a great book. Living the good life that God created you to live is not about getting even. Instead, we should look for opportunities to bless people, not curse them. This is the life of mercy and compassion God invites us to live.

In a scene from Victor Hugo's novel "Les Misérables," protagonist Jean Valjean steals silver from a compassionate priest. Instead of turning Jean into the authorities, the man says, "Here, take the rest!" **Ask God to show you one way you can exercise this kind of compassion to share the good life with a friend or a family member. As you pray, consider Jesus' words in verse 36 of today's text.**

DIG DEEPER

Read Luke 6:27-36 and meditate on what makes any compassion possible in the first place: God's mercy toward you. Invite God to keep this mercy for you in the forefront of your thoughts as you interact with others, especially those who seem undeserving of kindness. Journal your experience.

NOTES

WEEK 4 DAY 5 — Devotions
LUKE 15:18-20

18 I will set out and go back to my father and say to him: Father, I have sinned against heaven and against you. 19 I am no longer worthy to be called your son; make me like one of your hired servants. 20 So he got up and went to his father. But while he was still a long way off, his father saw him and was filled with compassion for him; he ran to his son, threw his arms around him and kissed him.

The parable of the lost son, perhaps the most famous of Jesus' parables, is a rich and beautiful story of restoration. Research and commentary abounds on this one sliver of the Bible. Today, in this small excerpt of the story, we will focus on the father's lavish compassion.

To understand the father's compassion, let's first examine the object of it: the son. When he decided to return home, it is hard to ascertain his feelings and motives. Is he remorseful? Does he genuinely feel sorry about disgracing and rejecting his father? Or perhaps he's putting on a show; he is so hungry and so tired of blowing up his life that he's willing to fake repentance and humility to enjoy his father's provision again.

In the father's mind, the son's motives do not seem to matter. Even though his son "was still a long way off," the father's compassion overflows. The son doesn't have to grovel at his father's feet; no penance is required. The father doesn't extend a chilly or passive aggressive welcome; he ran to his son, something quite undignified for a man of his status to do.

Take a minute to consider the phrase, "while he was still a long way off." Does it remind you of anyone you know? Maybe the phrase reminds you of yourself; is there anything keeping you from receiving God's welcome home? Talk to God about how you're feeling.

DIG DEEPER

Read Luke 15:11-32. Read the passage over a few times and imagine yourself in the story. What character do you most identify with: the father, the son or the older son? Why? Talk to God or journal about your experience.

NOTES

SMALL GROUP DISCUSSION GUIDE

> *COURAGE IS THE HABIT OF CHOOSING TO DO WHAT IS RIGHT EVEN WHEN YOU ARE AFRAID, ALONE, OUTNUMBERED OR FACE OVERWHELMING ODDS.*

THE GOOD LIFE: LIVING A LIFE OF COURAGE

Begin to discuss this week whether or not you'd like to continue to meet as a group together.

ICEBREAKER

Name a character in a movie, TV show or book or a person in real life who embodies the quality of courage for you. What makes him or her that way?

WATCH THE VIDEO

TEACHING OUTLINE

I. Following Christ is always a _____.

    A. You never come to a place of coasting as a Christ-follower.

    B. Daniel's age didn't stop him from being courageous.

II. Courage lives for something _____.

    A. God wants us to be willing to live a life of courage and impact.

    B. Courage takes the uncommon road.

III. Courage is not a matter of immediate inspiration; it is a habit.

    A. Continually orienting your _____ toward God.

    B. Continually seeking God in prayer.

    C. Continually obeying in the small areas of life.

IV. Courage will be _____.

BLANKS: *challenge, bigger, heart, tested*

DISCUSSION QUESTIONS

1. Do you have any people who have modeled courage in your life? Do you agree with Rich's definition of courage: "Courage is the habit of choosing to do what's right even when you are afraid, alone, outnumbered or face overwhelming odds." Why or why not?

READ DANIEL 6:1-23

2. What do you think Daniel might have been feeling as he read the decree? What thoughts could you imagine went through his head?

   What did Daniel stand to lose? (verse 3)

3. What is Daniel's response after the decree was made? How do you think you would have responded? Would you be willing to share?

4. What was the King's response? Do you think this was the right decision? Why or why not?

5. Rich states that courage is not something that just happens in an instant – it is a product of small choices and habits we have formed over time. How do you believe courage is formed?

   What is encouraging or discouraging about the idea that courage is formed over time?

6. Think of some examples of small steps or habits that could lead a person to make courageous choices – choosing to do what's right even when you are afraid, alone, outnumbered or face overwhelming odds.

   Name some habits or small choices that have led you to a courageous decision.

MINISTRY TIME

Spend a few minutes waiting in silence for God. Remember not to rush this time – we expect that God wants to connect with us today. Lead out with a prayer like: "Holy Spirit come and speak to us. We want you to fill us with courage."

Ask if anyone would like to receive prayer for courage. If there are a few people, have the group gather around and pray for them. Or break down into groups of 2-3 and pray for each other for any prayer needs.

NOTES

WEEK 5 DAY 1 Devotions
ACTS 5:27-29

27 The apostles were brought in and made to appear before the Sanhedrin to be questioned by the high priest. 28 "We gave you strict orders not to teach in this name," he said. "Yet you have filled Jerusalem with your teaching and are determined to make us guilty of this man's blood." 29 Peter and the other apostles replied: "We must obey God rather than human beings!"

Follow the rules and obey authority figures. These are values found in most cultures across the globe. They are instilled in children from a very young age, often to a fault. We disrespectfully tell children, "It's a rule because I said so. Don't question it!" Regarding authority figures, some kids are led to believe that obeying them must happen at any cost; even abuse and exploitation.

Take the magnitude of these cultural values in today's world and multiply it many times over. That's the environment the persecuted apostles were steeped in when they were dragged into court. In a culture where Pharisees, the most admired religious people, were known for strict adherence to thousands of rules and social norms and where anything less than complete deference to the high priest would get you in serious trouble, here were the apostles. And what did they do when the court ordered them to stop talking about Jesus? They responded, "We must obey God rather than human beings!"

It takes incredible courage to stand up to authority figures and to defy social norms. Maybe your boss is subtly suggesting you do "whatever it takes" to win a client because if you lose the client, you lose your job. Will you refuse to comply? If you do, you're disobeying an authority figure, which is not something that garners much approval in our society. Perhaps one friend often gossips about another. Will you contribute to the gossip? Refusing to do so will likely cause some embarrassment for your friend, a violation of a social norm. In moments like these, the courageous thing to do is to "obey God rather than human beings."

What is one area of your life where people's expectations of you conflict with the good life God created you to live? Someone or some institution wants you to do something but you know in your heart that it's not what God wants you to do. Pray that in these situations you would be able to courageously say "yes" to what God wants for you.

DIG DEEPER

Read Acts 5:17-42. The apostles showed courage at every opportunity. As you go about your day, think of it as a chance to practice doing what the apostles did by asking God to give you many clear opportunities to choose to do the right thing.

NOTES

WEEK 5 DAY 2 — Devotions
MATTHEW 26:38-39

38 Then he said to them, "My soul is overwhelmed with sorrow to the point of death. Stay here and keep watch with me." 39 Going a little farther, he fell with his face to the ground and prayed, "My Father, if it is possible, may this cup be taken from me. Yet not as I will, but as you will."

Yesterday, we examined the courageous act of doing the right thing in defiance of culturally constructed norms, when doing so may get you thrown into prison or physically harmed. At the very least, it causes social humiliation. Nonetheless, it requires bravery. Today, we will look at courage from a unique angle: a time when a man knew exactly what was going to happen; he knew he was going to die a gruesome death. This text from Matthew gives us a picture of Jesus in his final hours of life. Even though Jesus was all-knowing because he was fully God, he was also fully human. And in his humanity, he was terrified of the path that lay before him.

Jesus didn't promise that we would be spared from such fear, but he did promise a full life. Part of living the good life is knowing that in times of fear or hurt we are not alone. That means we are honored with the opportunity to be courageous and present with our friends when they are facing the seemingly insurmountable. This is why Jesus asked his friends to "stay here and keep watch." Friendships and meaningful community help us to be courageous.

Shift your focus to Jesus' prayer in this text. He asks God for a plan B, for anything but death on the cross. But then he goes on to surrender his will to his Father in heaven. Jesus did what was right when he was afraid; he placed his life in God's hands. Courage is not an absence of fear; it is admitting your fears but doing the right thing anyway. **What scares you about the world, your future, your family, etc.? Take some time now to admit your fears to God. Is there a friend you could invite into your fears to help you have courage?**

DIG DEEPER

Read Matthew 26:36-46. Jesus' friends dropped the ball several times. What do you need from God in order to be someone who faithfully keeps watch when others are afraid?

NOTES

WEEK 5 DAY 3 — Devotions
LUKE 5:18-19

18 Some men came carrying a paralyzed man on a mat and tried to take him into the house to lay him before Jesus. 19 When they could not find a way to do this because of the crowd, they went up on the roof and lowered him on his mat through the tiles into the middle of the crowd, right in front of Jesus.

Yesterday we spent some time considering how we can help our loved ones to be courageous. But what about doing courageous things for our loved ones? In this passage from the gospel of Luke, we read about friends who would stop at nothing to give their paralyzed friend a chance to encounter Jesus.

After you've mustered a lot of courage to try something outside of your comfort zone, you may not have much resolve left in order to keep going when setbacks come. You may be tempted to give up and never try again. When you feel this way, the men depicted in these verses set an inspiring example: they did whatever it took to get their friend directly in front of Jesus.

People who embrace the good life – those who live the life God created them to live – keep doing the right thing and don't give up whenever obstacles present themselves. What motivates them to do so? It's not to show off. Rather, the kind of courage God esteems is rooted in a love for others and in a desire to please God, even when you're afraid or the odds are stacked against you.

Perhaps you are afraid to pray for a sick friend. Maybe you hesitate to talk to a family member about Jesus. Perhaps you don't serve the poor because you fear for your safety. **What keeps you from stepping out of your comfort zone to help a friend or someone in need? Talk to God about these roadblocks and ask that his love would fill you up and give you the strength you need to overcome any hesitations.**

DIG DEEPER

Read Luke 5:17-26. Contrast the paralyzed man's friends with the Pharisees and teachers. The former were courageous for the sake of love; they pursued the good life. The latter were hardened by cynicism and obsession with rules, thus forsaking the life God wanted them to live. In what ways do you see yourself acting like the man's friends? What about the Pharisees; when are you prone to act like them?

NOTES

Devotions
DANIEL 3:16-18

16 Shadrach, Meshach and Abednego replied to him, "King Nebuchadnezzar, we do not need to defend ourselves before you in this matter. 17 If we are thrown into the blazing furnace, the God we serve is able to deliver us from it, and he will deliver us from Your Majesty's hand. 18 But even if he does not, we want you to know, Your Majesty, that we will not serve your gods or worship the image of gold you have set up."

We face overwhelming odds in this life. There are seasons when the very real possibility of death, danger or great loss overwhelm us and our loved ones. You've spent years trying to get pregnant and are convinced it's never going to happen. Your spouse had an affair; there's no way your marriage can be saved. You graduate college with a mountain of student loan debt; and you can't find a job. Your twenty-something child is checking into rehab, for the third time. These are the scary, insurmountable blazing furnaces of life.

Part of the courageous life is admitting that no matter how brave you are in a specific situation, you may not get what you want. God can intervene, but it may not look the way you want it to. You might not ever get pregnant. Your marriage may end. You might not be able to pay back the loans. Your child may never subdue her addictions. Shadrach, Meshach and Abednego understood this hard truth because they had a long history with God and recognized his goodness time and time again in their lives. Courageously, knowing they may not be delivered from the blazing furnace, they refused to worship anyone but God. When you face overwhelming odds and worst-case scenarios, the most courageous thing you can do is continue to allow God to be in charge of your life. What does this look like? It means you worship God through all of life's storms.

Worshipping God through these storms isn't a matter of putting on a fake smile and showing up at church to sing songs. God wants to give you so much more than that! He wants you to sense his presence and his comfort through even the lowest times. No matter how overwhelming your situation, he wants you to keep coming to him via prayer and community with other Christians. He even wants to give you peace and joy in the midst of your hardship. It seems impossible, but it's true; you can still experience the good life even when life feels anything but good!

With that in mind, what "blazing furnace" or worst-case scenarios are before you today? Write down some of the things that come to mind and bring them before God. Ask him to reveal one specific way you can continue to worship him and experience closeness with him as you face these "blazing furnaces."

DIG DEEPER

Read all of Daniel 3. Shadrach, Meshach and Abednego's courage to do the right thing had several outcomes: they survived the furnace, they were promoted and Nebuchadnezzar acknowledged the power of God. Remember times in your life that you were courageous and did the right thing and God's blessing came as a result. Journal your thanks to God.

NOTES

WEEK 5 — DAY 5: Devotions
EPHESIANS 6:13

13 Therefore put on the full armor of God, so that when the day of evil comes, you may be able to stand your ground, and after you have done everything, to stand.

Retreating and running far away is so tempting when you sense you're losing; when regaining what was lost seems impossible. However, in battle, especially in Biblical times, retreating is considered cowardly. Because of his love for you, God wants to give you everything you will need when you face these hard times.

Struggles in America are rarely ones of literal warfare, but the battles we face are definitely real. This verse from Paul's letter to the Ephesians speaks to this. There's a spiritual war happening all around us. Amidst battles where evil tries to thwart God's good intentions for your life; we must be courageous. But what does this look like? Oftentimes, rather than mounting a substantial counterattack, the bravest thing we can do is stand and hold our ground. Thanks to God, it's not by our own power that we courageously remain standing; it's by the protective power of his armor.

For some people, it's hard to ask for help and to fully rely on someone else. Perhaps you come from a family that prides itself on self-reliance, and you learned from a young age never to ask for help. If that's you, maybe the bravest thing you can do today is explicitly admit you need the power and protection of God's armor. There are simply too many battles and they are too hard to fight on your own. **Invite God into these battles. Try saying out loud that you need God and that you need his help to be courageous. Visualize yourself standing strong in life's battles, not retreating. How does this make you feel? What else do you want to say to God about it?**

DIG DEEPER

Read Ephesians 6:10-17. Paul describes all the garments of the armor of God coming together to help someone courageously resist evil. Beyond warfare garb, what other imagery speaks to your heart about God's power over evil? Perhaps there's something from nature, music, literature or sports that makes it come alive for you. Write down whatever comes to mind and revisit this imagery whenever you need to be courageous.

NOTES

SMALL GROUP DISCUSSION GUIDE

> *IT IS IMPOSSIBLE TO THINK OF LIVING A GOOD LIFE WITHOUT THINKING ABOUT CELEBRATION, ABOUT PARTIES, AND ABOUT A LIFE THAT'S FULL OF JOY.*

THE GOOD LIFE: LIVING A LIFE OF CELEBRATION

ICEBREAKER

What is the best birthday present you ever received?

WATCH THE VIDEO

TEACHING OUTLINE

I. Jesus modeled celebration

    A. Large parties like the one at Matthew's house.

    B. Seven-day wedding feasts.

    C. Celebration of Jewish holidays.

II. Jesus' _____ brought about celebration

    A. Shepherds celebrate.

    B. Angels celebrate.

    C. Unborn baby John the Baptist celebrates.

III. Stories of celebration from Jesus

    A. The shepherd seeks out a lost sheep.

        1. God _____ people before they _____ him.

        2. God is not content with those who have stayed close.

    B. Woman searches and cleans for her _____.

        1. God highly values us.

        2. God rejoices over a relationship with us and wants to share that with us.

BLANKS: *arrival, seeks, seek, coin*

DISCUSSION QUESTIONS

1. What are your favorite celebrations of the year? What makes them meaningful to you?

READ LUKE 15:8-10

2. Have you ever lost anything really important to you? Describe your experience.

3. What is your image of Jesus? Do you picture him laughing or joyful? Why or why not?

4. Rich talks about four different ways that the church relates to people far from God:

    - They despise them.

    - They are indifferent.

    - They only welcome those who first come seeking.

    - They actively look for people far from God to welcome in.

    Which of these ways do you think the church approaches people far from God? How would it impact people far from God if the church universally took the fourth approach?

5. Rich says there is nothing in the world's religions that tells of a God who initiates a search for people who are not interested in him. How does it make you feel that there is a God who is seeking you out?

MINISTRY TIME

Pray and invite God to speak to you and your group. Take a few minutes of silence and consider Rich's last point: "Whenever we turn to God after having our backs toward him, he celebrates and invites us into his celebration." Is there anyone in the group that feels like their back is toward God and they want to turn toward him? Pray for them to feel God's joy.

Take a few minutes to close the group with a prayer of thanks for these six weeks of being together! It's important to celebrate that you completed this six-week study together. Make a plan to connect in the next few weeks and gather at someone's home, restaurant, park, etc., and celebrate what God has done through this small group.

NOTES

WEEK 6 DAY 1 — Devotions
2 SAMUEL 6:21-22

21 David said to Michal, "It was before the LORD, who chose me rather than your father or anyone from his house when he appointed me ruler over the LORD's people Israel – I will celebrate before the LORD. 22 I will become even more undignified than this, and I will be humiliated in my own eyes. But by these slave girls you spoke of, I will be held in honor."

Different cultures party differently. Imagine a wedding where the bride and groom come from different ethnic backgrounds. Perhaps you've witnessed such a union or this describes your own wedding day. One side of the aisle sits quietly during the ceremony, not emoting much. Meanwhile, the other side is lively, audibly praising the beautiful bride and calling-and-responding to the pastor throughout the homily.

We all have a line. Depending on your upbringing, ethnicity, temperament, etc., it will fall somewhere on a spectrum, but the line exists nonetheless. On the acceptable side of the line, you're relaxed and enjoying the celebration. But then you cross the line, perhaps from drinking to excess, and you become "undignified" and "humiliated."

When celebrating, is it ever worth it to become undignified and to humiliate yourself? In this text from the Old Testament book of 2 Samuel, Kind David of Israel deviates from social expectations of royal behavior and any sense of propriety in order to celebrate God. He doesn't care what his wife thinks; he doesn't care what anyone but God thinks. He hasn't had one too many drinks; he's not limiting himself to celebrating in a way that reflects his upbringing. He is undone, ecstatic, overflowing with gratitude, and so happy to celebrate his Lord and his God, no matter how undignified it makes him look.

It is possible to posture yourself in this way and to live this life of celebration. You can freely sing, dance, shout, move, respond or create in ways that reflect your gratitude and the joy you find in God. **Today, when you are alone, put on some music, paint or draw, go for a walk in nature or read a poem (a psalm from the Bible would be a great choice). As you do this, try just one of the above-mentioned expressions of worship and resist any temptation to be uptight or self-conscious about it. How does it feel to celebrate God in this unrestrained way?**

DIG DEEPER

Read all of 2 Samuel 6. Trace all the instances of David and others celebrating God "with all their might." How does this story further inspire you to live the good life of celebration?

NOTES

WEEK 6 DAY 2 — Devotions
LUKE 15:3-7

3 Then Jesus told them this parable: 4 "Suppose one of you has a hundred sheep and loses one of them. Doesn't he leave the ninety-nine in the open country and go after the lost sheep until he finds it? 5 And when he finds it, he joyfully puts it on his shoulders 6 and goes home. Then he calls his friends and neighbors together and says, 'Rejoice with me; I have found my lost sheep.' 7 I tell you that in the same way there will be more rejoicing in heaven over one sinner who repents than over ninety-nine righteous persons who do not need to repent."

In this final week we revisit the way the Bible often uses shepherd imagery to describe God, as we did during the first week. Jesus offers us insight into the relationship between a shepherd and his sheep when he says in John 10, "no one will snatch them out of my hand." We see this illustrated in the Old Testament when the young shepherd David bravely fought a lion and a bear to protect his flock. When we see that level of investment, we begin to understand how deep the love of God our Shepherd is for us. And when we understand how deeply that love runs, is it any surprise that when we are returned to our Shepherd he is overcome with joy, and invites everyone who loves him to come and celebrate with him?

In this parable from Luke the shepherd leaves 99 sheep with some other shepherds to seek out his one lost sheep. Later, upon his return with the sheep, his friends rejoice with him. Friends of God rejoice and celebrate when someone who was lost is found. They celebrate even when the process is messy, awkward, takes a long time or feels like one step forward, two steps back. They celebrate because they love God and because his love for them is so abundant that it pours out onto everyone around them. However, sometimes we are so hyper-focused on our own efforts, victories and struggles that we lose sight of what God is doing in the lives of our friends and our families.

When we make efforts to see those around us as deeply loved children of God, we see that their little victories are actually not so little at all. When our friends are making more choices that orient them toward a life that looks like Jesus', like the good life God created them to live, what might seem inconsequential to many is a matter of great significance and appreciation for us. God desires us to join him in rejoicing and celebrating with and for others; he wants his friends to come to the party. A life eager to celebrate those around you is indeed a good life. **This week, find one person or situation to celebrate. How does it feel to celebrate others and cheer them on?**

DIG DEEPER

Read Luke 15:8-10. This parable follows that of the lost sheep. What sticks out to you in these two stories? What might be Jesus' invitation to you in these parables?

NOTES

Devotions
LUKE 15:22-24

22 But the father said to his servants, "Quick! Bring the best robe and put it on him. Put a ring on his finger and sandals on his feet. 23 Bring the fattened calf and kill it. Let's have a feast and celebrate. 24 For this son of mine was dead and is alive again; he was lost and is found." So they began to celebrate.

Pizza on paper plates alongside cheap beer may be the way we typically gather and celebrate in America today, but elsewhere in the world, hosts reserve the choicest fare for parties and lavish luxurious treatment on their guests. We see it here in the parable of the lost son, found in Luke 15, like yesterday's text. It's a chapter in the Bible that tells us so much about a life of celebration. The father puts his best robe on his son and orders a huge quantity of the finest food to be prepared. The son expects to return to his father's household a servant at best, but his dad fully celebrates and restores him as his son.

When you host a party, it's often to honor a loved one's special milestone, such as a graduation. Now, imagine a completely different reason to celebrate: throwing a giant party for your thieving, drug-addicted son when he decides to come home after months of reckless living. In his book, "The Kingdom of God is a Party," pastor Tony Campolo describes an experience when, jet lagged and hungry, he finds himself at a grungy diner at 3 a.m. When a group of prostitutes enter after concluding their night's work, he overhears one of the women tell another that her birthday is the following day and that she's never had a birthday party. Tony decides to throw a surprise birthday party for the woman the following night. He decorates the diner from wall-to-wall, the owner makes a cake, and seemingly all the prostitutes in town show up for the surprise. When Agnes, the guest of honor walks in, she is stunned by the great celebration and act of love.

These are pictures of how God celebrates us even when we don't deserve it. His love goes so deep for us; we cannot even imagine! **Ask God for a deeper understanding of how much he celebrates and welcomes you into his family, despite anything you might have done that makes you think you don't deserve love. How can you take this amazing way God has given you the good life and share it with others?**

DIG DEEPER

Read Luke 15:11-32, the entire parable of the lost son. You were given an opportunity to do this a few weeks ago, when considering the life of compassion. When you look at the text with a life of celebration in mind, what jumps out at you?

NOTES

WEEK 6 DAY 4 — Devotions
JOHN 16:20-22

20 Very truly I tell you, you will weep and mourn while the world rejoices. You will grieve, but your grief will turn to joy. 21 A woman giving birth to a child has pain because her time has come; but when her baby is born she forgets the anguish because of her joy that a child is born into the world. 22 So with you: Now is your time of grief, but I will see you again and you will rejoice, and no one will take away your joy.

As we've looked through the scriptures this week to glimpse how celebration is part of living the good life, you may feel like you didn't get an invitation to the party. You are not celebrating; you are weeping and grieving. You buried your mother this year. You have countless bills in collections. Your fiancé broke off the engagement. The celebratory good life God wants you to live feels out of your reach.

The world around you celebrates holidays, sports teams, good weather and the weekend while you silently suffer the end of your marriage, a miscarriage or the loss of a job. Jesus doesn't want you to deny, self-medicate or suppress this suffering. He plainly says to us, "Now is your time of grief." God doesn't want you to pretend like everything's OK. He wants to stand with you and acknowledge your hurts. Psalm 34:18 says, "The Lord is close to the brokenhearted and saves those who are crushed in spirit." God wants to meet you in the grief and hold you while you do the ugly cry. He wants to carry the burden for you.

Sometimes, after the ugly cry, the morning comes. We taste heaven and its accompanying joy in the dawn of a new day. There are moments where the weight of things feels lifted. We may experience the freedom of taking dark things and sadness into the light. This is the experience of one of the Bible's promises: God's mercies are new every morning. They are appetizers of the feast of heavenly joy Jesus talks about in verse 22: "I will see you again and you will rejoice, and no one will take away your joy." No matter what your hurt or grief, God will present you with opportunities throughout your life to experience and celebrate even the tiniest bit of this joy.

If you are in a "time of grief," invite God to still give you the joy and celebration of eternity. Give thanks to God for this hope of heaven and its ability to break into our lives today. If you are not in a time of grief, ask God to show you how to come alongside someone else in their time of pain.

DIG DEEPER

Read John 16:16-33. The disciples are puzzled by Jesus' words in verse 16. This prompts him to offer a fuller explanation, which bolsters his followers' faith, as seen in verse 30. What about Jesus puzzles you? Is there anything in your life right now that doesn't make sense? Invite Jesus to speak to you about these matters; journal any thoughts you might have.

NOTES

WEEK 6 DAY 5 — Devotions
REVELATION 7:9-10

9 After this I looked, and there before me was a great multitude that no one could count, from every nation, tribe, people and language, standing before the throne and before the Lamb. They were wearing white robes and were holding palm branches in their hands. 10 And they cried out in a loud voice: "Salvation belongs to our God, who sits on the throne, and to the Lamb."

Fittingly, we finish this six-week reflection on the good life, the one God created us to live, in the book of Revelation, the very last book in the Bible. This book about the end of the world has long fascinated, frightened, confused and emboldened believers and non-believers alike. It is legendary! In these verses from chapter 7, the author John is describing celebrations in heaven.

Focus on the phrase "a great multitude" and its accompanying description: every nation, tribe, people and language. This is a wonderful reason to celebrate: together, with different people from all over the world, we can proclaim the goodness of God, his healing and redemption of the entire world, both now and forevermore. It's the greatest party the world has ever known and everyone is invited! Let's celebrate! Instead of fearing or despising people who look different, who speak a different language, or who have different cultural values, we should celebrate God with them.

There are a few other noteworthy things about the "great multitude" of people in this text: they are wearing white robes and holding palm branches. These are markers of celebration, found elsewhere in the Bible. In John 12, when Jesus enters Jerusalem, people hold palm branches, a symbol of God's salvation, and proclaim, "O save!" This event in Jesus' life is commemorated by Christians all over the world every year on Palm Sunday, the Sunday before Easter.

Also in John 12, exasperated Pharisees observe the scene and proclaim, "Look how the whole world has gone after him!" This is one of the few important things the Pharisees, the super religious but misguided people of Jesus' day, were actually right about: the whole world does indeed go after Jesus and we see the culmination of it here in Revelation 7. We should remark as the Pharisees do, but in celebration, not exasperation. Jesus is the king; he is the savior of the world and the one who longs to give everyone the good life! We can join with people across the globe to celebrate his goodness for all of eternity! **Ask God for one idea that will allow you to "go after" Jesus and celebrate him alongside people who are different than you. How will you begin to walk this out?**

DIG DEEPER

Read Revelation 7:9-17. This is quite the spectacle. What excites you about this passage? What makes you most want to celebrate?

NOTES

Thank you for participating. We hope this journey has been fruitful.

For more resources, please visit **vineyardcolumbus.org**.